Francis Frith's

Essex Coast
Photographic Memories

Russell Thompson was born in Chelmsford in 1965. He was
educated at the town's Grammar School, and subsequently at St
Martin's School of Art in Covent Garden. He currently works in
adult education, as a Creative Writing teacher. At other times, he
is a regular performer on London's poetry and cabaret circuits.

Francis Frith's

Essex Coast
Photographic Memories

Russell Thompson

www.francisfrith.com

First published in the United Kingdom in 2001 by The Francis Frith Collection.

Hardback edition published in 2001 ISBN 1-85937-342-9

Reprinted in paperback 2009 ISBN 978-1-84589-448-1

British Library Cataloguing in Publication Data

Francis Frith's Essex Coast - Photographic Memories
Russell Thompson
ISBN 978-1-84589-448-1

The Francis Frith Collection
Frith's Barn, Teffont,
Salisbury, Wiltshire SP3 5QP
Tel: +44 (0) 1722 716 376
Email: info@francisfrith.co.uk
www.francisfrith.com

Printed and bound in Malta

Front Cover: **Canvey Island, The Beach c1955** C237065t

The colour-tinting is for illustrative purposes only, and is not intended to be historically accurate

Aerial photographs reproduced under licence from Simmons Aerofilms Limited.
Every attempt has been made to contact copyright holders of illustrative material. We will be happy to give full
acknowledgement in future editions for any items not credited.
Any information should be directed to The Francis Frith Collection.

AS WITH ANY HISTORICAL DATABASE THE FRITH ARCHIVE IS CONSTANTLY BEING CORRECTED AND IMPROVED AND
THE PUBLISHERS WOULD WELCOME INFORMATION ON OMISSIONS OR INACCURACIES

Essex Coast
Photographic Memories

Contents

Hunstanton, The Beach From the Pier 1927 79727

FRANCIS FRITH

Victorian Pioneer

FRANCIS FRITH, founder of the world-famous photographic archive, was a complex and multi-talented man. A devout Quaker and a highly successful Victorian businessman, he was philosophical by nature and pioneering in outlook.

By 1855 he had established a wholesale grocery business in Liverpool, and sold it for the astonishing sum of £200,000, which is the equivalent today of over £15,000,000. Now a very rich man, he was able to indulge his passion for travel. As a child he had pored over travel books written by early explorers, and his fancy and imagination had been stirred by family holidays to the sublime mountain regions of Wales and Scotland. 'What lands of spirit-stirring and enriching scenes and places!' he had written. He was to return to these scenes of grandeur in later years to 'recapture the thousands of vivid and tender memories', but with a different purpose. Now in his thirties, and captivated by the new science of photography,

Frith set out on a series of pioneering journeys up the Nile and to the Near East that occupied him from 1856 until 1860.

Intrigue and Exploration

These far-flung journeys were packed with intrigue and adventure. In his life story, written when he was sixty-three, Frith tells of being held captive by bandits, and of fighting 'an awful midnight battle to the very point of surrender with a deadly pack of hungry, wild dogs'. Wearing flowing Arab costume, Frith arrived at Akaba by camel sixty years before Lawrence of Arabia, where he encountered 'desert princes and rival sheikhs, blazing with jewel-hilted swords'.

He was the first photographer to venture beyond the sixth cataract of the Nile. Africa was still the mysterious 'Dark Continent', and Stanley and Livingstone's historic meeting was a decade into the future. The conditions for picture taking confound belief. He laboured for hours in his wicker dark-room in the sweltering heat of the desert, while the volatile chemicals fizzed dangerously in their trays. Back in London he exhibited his photographs and was 'rapturously cheered' by members of the Royal Society. His reputation as a photographer was made overnight.

Venture of a Life-Time

Characteristically, Frith quickly spotted the opportunity to create a new business as a specialist publisher of photographs. He lived in an era of immense and sometimes violent change. For the poor in the early part of Victoria's reign work was exhausting and the hours long, and people had precious little free time to enjoy themselves. Most had no transport

other than a cart or gig at their disposal, and rarely travelled far beyond the boundaries of their own town or village. However, by the 1870s the railways had threaded their way across the country, and Bank Holidays and half-day Saturdays had been made obligatory by Act of Parliament. All of a sudden the working man and his family were able to enjoy days out and see a little more of the world.

With typical business acumen, Francis Frith foresaw that these new tourists would enjoy having souvenirs to commemorate their days out. In 1860 he married Mary Ann Rosling and set out on a new career: his aim was to photograph every city, town and village in Britain. For the next thirty years he travelled the country by train and by pony and trap, producing fine photographs of seaside resorts and beauty spots that were keenly bought by millions of Victorians. These prints were painstakingly pasted into family albums and pored over during the dark nights of winter, rekindling precious memories of summer excursions.

The Rise of Frith & Co

Frith's studio was soon supplying retail shops all over the country. To meet the demand he gathered about him a small team of photographers, and published the work of

independent artist-photographers of the calibre of Roger Fenton and Francis Bedford. In order to gain some understanding of the scale of Frith's business one only has to look at the catalogue issued by Frith & Co in 1886: it runs to some 670 pages, listing not only many thousands of views of the British Isles but also many photographs of most European countries, and China, Japan, the USA and Canada. By 1890 Frith had created the greatest specialist photographic publishing company in the world, with over 2,000 sales outlets - more than the combined number that Boots and WH Smith have today! The picture on page 7 shows the Frith & Co display board at Ingleton in the Yorkshire Dales (left of window). Beautifully constructed with a mahogany frame and gilt inserts, it could display up to a dozen local scenes.

Postcard Bonanza

The ever-popular holiday postcard we know today took many years to develop. In 1870 the Post Office issued the first plain cards, with a pre-printed stamp on one face. In 1894 they allowed other publishers' cards to be sent through the mail with an attached adhesive halfpenny stamp. Demand grew rapidly, and in 1895 a new size of postcard was permitted called the court card, but there was little room for illustration. In 1899, a year after Frith's death, a new card measuring 5.5 x 3.5 inches became the standard format, but it was not until 1902 that the divided back came into being, so that the address and message could be on one face and a full-size illustration on the other. Frith & Co were in the vanguard of postcard development: Frith's sons Eustace and Cyril continued their father's monumental task, expanding the number of views offered to the public and recording more and more places in Britain, as the coasts and countryside were opened up to mass travel.

Francis Frith had died in 1898 at his villa in Cannes, his great project still growing. The archive he created continued in business for another seventy years. By 1970 it contained over a third of a million pictures showing 7,000 British towns and villages.

Francis Frith's Legacy

Frith's legacy to us today is of immense significance and value, for the magnificent archive of evocative photographs he created provides a unique record of change in the cities, towns and villages throughout Britain over a century and more. Frith and his fellow studio photographers revisited locations many times down the years to update their views, compiling for us an enthralling and colourful pageant of British life and character.

We are fortunate that Frith was dedicated to recording the minutiae of everyday life, for it is this sheer wealth of visual data, the painstaking chronicle of changes in dress, transport, street layouts, buildings, housing, engineering and landscape that captivates us so much today. His remarkable images offer us a powerful link with the past and with the lives of our ancestors.

The Value of the Archive Today

Computers have now made it possible for Frith's many thousands of images to be accessed almost instantly. Frith's images are increasingly used as visual resources, by social historians, by researchers into genealogy and ancestry, by architects and town planners, and by teachers involved in local history projects.

In addition, the archive offers every one of us an opportunity to examine the places where we and our families have lived and worked down the years. Highly successful in Frith's own era, the archive is now, a century and more on, entering a new phase of popularity. Historians consider the Francis Frith Collection to be of prime national importance. It is the only archive of its kind remaining in private ownership. Francis Frith's archive is now housed in an historic timber barn in the beautiful village of Teffont in Wiltshire. Its founder would not recognize the archive office as it is today. In place of the many thousands of dusty boxes containing glass plate negatives and an all-pervading odour of photographic chemicals, there are now ranks of computer screens. He would be amazed to watch his images travelling round the world at unimaginable speeds through internet lines.

The archive's future is both bright and exciting. Francis Frith, with his unshakeable belief in making photographs available to the greatest number of people, would undoubtedly approve of what is being done today with his lifetime's work. His photographs depicting our shared past are now bringing pleasure and enlightenment to millions around the world a century and more after his death.

Wicken Bonant
Debden
Clavering
Rictding
Widdington
Little Sampford
Finchingfield
Hedingham
Sible Hedingham
Berdon
Quendon
THAXTED
Little Bardfield
Blackwater
Weathersfield
Ugley
Henham on the Hill
Chickney
Great Bardfield
Shalford
Gosfield
Pledgen
Broxted
Tilty
Lindsell
Bardfield Saling
Boking
Manewden
Benfield
Elsenham
Great Easton
Great Saling
Farnham
Stansted Mountfitchet
Little Easton
Stebbing
Panfield
Rayne
BRAINTRE
Birchanger
Takeley
Churchend
DUNMOW
Lit Canfield
BISHOP STORTFORD
Lit Dunmow
Feelstead
Great Hallingbury
River
Barnston
Black Notley
Little Hallingbury
Great Canfield
High Roothing
Chelmer
Chailey
Lit Leighs
Whits Notle
Hatfield Broad Oak
Aythorpe Roothing
High Easter
Pleshey
Fairsted
Gr: Leighs
Fanlk
Riv Ter
Sheering
White Roothing
Barwick
Leaden Roothing
Good Easter
Gr: Waltham
Terling
Little Parndon
Matching
Margaret Roothing
Mashbury
Lit Waltham
HODDESDON
Harlow
Abbots Roothing
Chignall Smealy
Broomfield
Roydon
Latton
Berners Roothing
Chignall St James
Boreham
Great Parndon
Netswell
Little Laver
Beauchamp Roothing
Roxwell
Springfield
Nazeing
Laver Magdalen
High Laver
Shellow Bowels
Willingale Doe
Mildmay
Lit Bad Wof
Rye Hill
Moreton
Fyfield
Willingale Spain
Writtle
Moulsham
Epping Upland
Bobbingworth
Shelley
Norton Mandeville
Widford
CHELMSFORD
Hollyfield
N. Weald Bassett
High Ongar
Great Baddow
Sandon
EPPING
Greenstead
CHIPPING ONGAR
WALTHAM ABBEY
Upshire
Stanford Rivers
Stondon Massey
Blackmore
Thoydon Garnon
Thoydon Mount
Kelvedon Hatch
Fryerning
Margaretting
W. Hanningfield
E. Han
Woodha
Seward stone
Thoydon Bois
Stapleford Tawney
Doddinghurst
Ingatestone
Stock
Loughton
Navestock
Buttsbury
S. Hanningfield
Ferr
Chingford
Lambourne
Mountnessing
Woodford
Stapleford Abbots Rivers
Shenfield
BELLERICAY
Ramsden Bellhouse
Downham
Rette
Walthamstow
Chigwell
St Weald
Hutton
Ramsden Crays
Runwell
Ra
Henhault Forest
Brentwood
Wickford
Wanstead
Chadwell
Havering atte Bower
Ingrave
G. Bursstead
Nevendon
N. Beuf
Thunders
Low Layton
ROMFORD
G. Warley
Lit Warley
Childerditch
Lit Bursstead
E. Horndon
Laindon
Basildon
Alford
Hornchurch
W. Horndon
Dunton
Pitsea
Bow
Lit Alford
Upminster
Cranham
Langdon Hills
Vange
Bowers Gifford
South Ben
West Ham
Barking
Dagenham
N. Ockendon
Bulphan
Horndon on the Hill
Fobbing
Corringham
Canvey Id
Cha
East Ham
Ripple
Rainham
S. Ockendon
Orsett
Standford le Hope
Mucking
RIVER
London
Lea
Wennington
Avely
Stifford
Chadwell
West Tilbury
Little Lo
In Kent
THAMES RIVER
Purfleet
Lit Thurrock
GRAYS THURROCK
West Tilbury
East Tilbury
W. Thurrock
Tilbury Fort
K
E
GRAVESEND
N
T

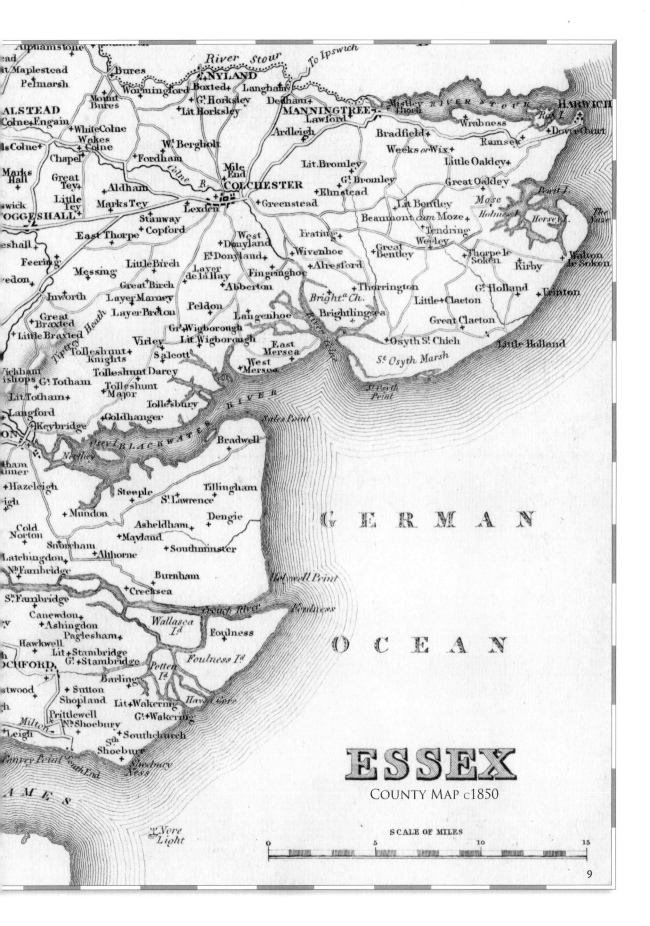

ESSEX

COUNTY MAP c1850

SCALE OF MILES

0   5   10   15

Essex Coast - An Introduction

One of the formative experiences of my early life was the discovery of a battered 1-inch Ordnance Survey map in the glove box of the family car. It covered the majority of the Essex coast, and included many places that were already familiar. After all, there had been no shortage of Sunday excursions to the Marine Lake at Maldon, or summer train-rides to Walton-on-the-Naze. But there was something else here, too - something that was unexpected, unguessed-at. Much of the excitement, it seemed, was in the shapes, as is so often the case with maps. There were wide blue estuaries, creeks pursuing strangely angular courses, and areas dotted with the 'tufty' symbols that meant 'marsh'. Elsewhere, vast peninsulas of land poked into the sea; in some places, it did not even seem entirely clear where the one ended and the other began. Then there were the islands - so many of them: oval Mersea, triangular Canvey, the knotty jigsaw of the Roach archipelago, and countless little slivers with names like Rat Island and Cindery Island. This was truly a revelation.

That particular map, it later transpired, had captured a version of the Essex coast that was already passing into history. But what a history it had been. Essex is frequently described as a county of contrasts, the sea being just one of its many aspects. Whilst this is perfectly valid, it is also true that the coast itself has a number of different facets: it brings livelihood, it provides leisure, it destroys. It teems with food and wildlife. It needs to be protected, and it needs to be protected against.

In the church at Brightlingsea, there are more than 200 memorial plaques, each one to a missing seafarer. They remind us of Essex's love-hate relationship with the sea, and they also remind us that this coast was heavily reliant on fishing. Villages like Leigh-on-Sea were almost wholly based upon it. Early photographs show fishing boats drawn up on Leigh's foreshore, and great piles of cockles like snowdrifts. Even the mighty Southend had begun life as a cluster of fishermen's cottages.

Shrimps, mussels and sole all were abundant here, but the main fruit of Essex's coastal waters was the oyster. A huge industry developed around it, culminating once a year in Colchester's semi-mystical Oyster Feast ceremony. Tiny

settlements like Paglesham depended on their oyster beds. The geological nature of the Essex coast, plus the equable temperature of its river mouths, meant that these were good breeding grounds. Unfortunately, the oyster suffered in the 20th century, as a result of disease and bad winters, and, despite sporadic revivals, the industry has never properly recovered.

Winters have sometimes destroyed more than just oysters. In the floods of January 1953, there were 58 deaths on Canvey Island and 35 at Jaywick. Parts of the Essex coast were simply too low-lying to cope with the high water. Wallasea Island, which was then mercifully under-populated, reportedly filled up "like a bowl" when its sea wall was breached. It is an ongoing problem; Jaywick has only recently been fitted with a colossal new breakwater of imported stone. It is also a very old problem. As early as the 1620s, a Dutch entrepreneur called Joas Croppenburg was called in to furnish Canvey with a serviceable sea wall, hence the island's early Dutch colony.

In 1667, an invasion fleet, also Dutch, paid a less neighbourly visit to the Essex coast. East Tilbury church got in the way of a stray cannonball and, to this day, has no tower. The fleet was thwarted, but the incident nonetheless highlighted another feature of the Essex coast: it is often the first landfall for hostile invaders.

The alderman Byrhtnoth (himself ultimately of Saxon stock) had learnt this to his cost when trying to repel marauding Danes at the Battle of Maldon in 991. Further south, Shoeburyness and Tilbury take their names from early coastal fortresses. And, belonging to a later age, we have the string of Martello towers that were installed to protect the shoreline of the Tendring peninsula from Napoleon. These days they sit innocuously beside golf links and caravan parks.

It is, indeed, more by leisure pursuits such as these, that many people now know the Essex coast. Southend and Clacton, certainly, have become bywords for a particular kind of British seaside experience. Visitors are now less likely to spend a fortnight's holiday in either town, yet they remain immensely popular places. Longer established than Clacton is Walton-on-the-Naze - a town of enormous charm, that "never quite made it" as a resort, in the words of one writer. One suspects that this has been its saving grace. Its neighbour Frinton, sealed off from the world by its level-crossing gates, presents yet another face of the British seaside. And so on.

It is strange to think that these resorts sprang from a late 18th-century fad for 'taking the waters'. Strange, too, to see photographs of bathing machines on sites that are now

occupied by funfairs of the grosser sort. After all, Southend's initial aim had been to attract "persons of the first rank and fashion" and "the genteelest company". Like Essex's other resorts, it was opened up, once and for all, by the railway.

It would seem that we could learn a lot about humanity in general, simply by looking at pictures of beach scenes. Piers that started out as blank jetties became gradually encrusted with shooting saloons, 'what-the-butler-saw' machines, and berths for passenger steamers. Bandstands appeared almost overnight, and were soon playing host to visiting German bands, whilst troupes of Pierrots performed end-of-pier shows several times a day.

In our trip around the coast, we should not forget the towns that were once, and in some cases still are, ports. It is true that the county's waterfront was not suited to large ports, because, with the exception of Harwich, there are no natural harbours. Yet Maldon, with its estuary connected to Chelmsford by a canal, was important for the shipment of coal and corn, whilst wool was exported from Burnham. Mistley, Manningtree, Wivenhoe and Brightlingsea were also involved in coastwise and continental trade. Grays shipped bricks and

chalk, and even humble quays like Bradwell's played their part.

Several of these towns boasted shipyards, too. Harwich was once home to a royal dockyard, and a number of men-of-war were constructed there between the 17th and early 19th centuries.

Essex's biggest port, when it arrived, was purpose-built. Tilbury Docks were deep enough for the very largest ships to enter or leave at high or low tide. They were the first Port Of London docks encountered by a ship sailing up the Thames. It was only a matter of time before Tilbury was accommodating passenger liners too. The 'Windrush' docked here in the late 1940s, and the docks became the gateway for new citizens from the Caribbean.

Inevitably, the Essex coast had also been party to more illicit forms of import. Facing the German Ocean, and crazy-paved with dykes and inlets, the landscape was ideal for smuggling purposes. Kegs or bales of contraband could be hidden in hummocks of grass out on the marshes. Sometimes it seems that every ancient pub within a stone's throw of the coast reputedly has the cubbyholes and passages that mark it out as a smugglers' den. It was certainly an activity that seemed

to unite the community - everybody was in on it. Oyster merchants and dredger men would use their boats for trafficking goods. It threw up some 'characters', too, such as Paglesham's churchwarden-smuggler William 'Hard Apple' Blyth, who was evidently a force to be reckoned with.

However, these are generalisations, and this book includes towns and villages whose features are their own and nobody else's. Hadleigh has its magnificent Castle, Horndon-on-the-Hill its Woolmarket. Stanford-le-Hope and Corringham have their oil refineries, Mistley its maltings, and Harwich and Dovercourt have their lighthouses (their 'leading lights').

Out on the big hoof of the Dengie peninsula, is Bradwell-on-Sea. There sits St Peter's Chapel, which was already four hundred years old at the time of the Norman Conquest. The fact that it was built on the foundations of a Roman shore-fort adds an extra degree of history to this wild part of the coast. And 'wild' is the operative word in some of these places. Standing outside St Peter's on a December afternoon, with the light failing and the grey sea coming in close, it is odd to think that you are only 45 miles from London Bridge. Can this really be the much-maligned Essex? Is this the county that, to many people, simply means Liverpool Street station?

Other things are prone to change, though, and some ways of life illustrated here have gone forever. For example, we no longer see brown-sailed hay barges racing each other up the Thames. We can no longer, presumably, hire a brougham in Clacton-on-Sea. That is the beauty of photography - it lends an immortality to things that otherwise do not last.

Still, the Essex coast is adaptable. It has had to weather far worse things than social and technological upheaval. These days, people visit The Stone for its water sport facilities; people venture onto Wallasea for the yachting. Whilst many of us would not wish to see the entire coast turned into one enormous marina, others argue that there is a need to revitalise places whose traditional livelihoods have disappeared. It is a problem.

Southend's seven-mile front does not bear much resemblance to its original fishing village, it is true; but holidaymakers have often been glad of the locally caught seafood on offer there. So there is often continuity, even if it is in something as intangible as the 'feel' of a place.

In this book, we go by the map; we travel northwards, from Grays to Manningtree. Sometimes we go by land, sometimes by water; the old duo. It is a vast coast, solid, but not too solid, and at the very least, it deserves our respect.

Southend-on-Sea From the Air 1938 AF58224

Grays
High Street c1955 G85015
In the 1950s wasp waists were in, hats were out and shopping baskets were still made of wicker. The High Street, seen here from the point where the level crossing cuts across it, is somewhat different today. It is now pedestrianised, and benches and small trees have been added. Many of the buildings have been replaced, though the ex-Woolworth's still remains.

▼ Grays

The Thames c1955 G85032

Long before Grays was an industrial town, it was a port, used by coastal traffic from London. Pepys, for instance, says that he once took a wherry to Grays and 'bought a great deal of fine fish'. In this picture, we see a small coastal motor vessel with derricks, and inshore, a cluster of lighters and barges.

▼ Grays, The Promenade c1955 G85006

In 1906 Grays acquired a large consignment of fine sand and opened a pleasure beach. It was nothing if not a bold move: there was a boating-lake, gardens and a swimming pool. The setting commanded a good view of the river; note the number of appreciative deckchair users here.

▲ Grays
The Lightship
c1955 G85034

The lightship did sterling service as a warning and navigation mark. Indeed, Thurrock and ships are intimately connected: the very place name means 'hull of a boat, where bilge collects'. Most experts, with great generosity of spirit, say this refers to the shape of the Thames at this point.

◄ **Tilbury**
The Thames c1960
T114008
A motor vessel, a steam tug, and an old 'island type' steamer pass on the river. Were it not for the Thames, of course, there would be no Tilbury. The famous Docks were opened in April 1886. As well as 100 acres of water, the original facilities included a hospital, a mission, a mortuary, and a steam laundry.

◄ **Tilbury**
The Ferry c1960

T114001

There has been a ferry between Tilbury and Gravesend since at least Roman times. The 'Rose', pictured here, is one of many boats to have run the service over the years. As well as the passenger ferry, vehicular traffic was catered for before the Dartford Tunnel opened. The current 'five minute crossing' is thoroughly recommended.

◄ Tilbury
The Ferry c1960

T114025

1,142 ft long, this floating landing stage was built in 1927, along with the two large buildings with cupolas. The one on the left was the customs baggage-hall, and on the right is a 'circulating area' for passengers en route between ships and trains. A grand five-storey hotel used to stand beyond the two buildings.

▼ Tilbury
Calcutta Road c1960

T114011

Soon after the Docks were opened, 'a considerable town' sprang up around them; note the derrick on the skyline. The road names recall the port's connection with distant parts of the Empire - Montreal Road, Canberra Square, and Calcutta Road. The young men around the 'Glo-Joy' board are sporting a variety of 'Edwardian' fashion.

◄ Tilbury
Civic Square c1960

T114019

There is still a 'druggist' at the corner today, though a betting shop has appeared on the site of the 'News of the World' vendor. Behind the war memorial are the town's civic buildings, such as administration departments and a library, which were built in 1924. Tilbury is now part of the new Thurrock unitary authority.

▼ Tilbury

War Memorial c1960 T114014

Tilbury's war memorial reads 'May Justice Mercy & Peace Prevail Among The Nations'. It includes names from Malaya (1950) and the Falklands (1982). On the right, J W Pigg & Sons, Grocers, were well known in Thurrock. They once had a fleet of horse-drawn carts (later vans) operating a delivery service to outlying areas.

▼ Tilbury

Fort Grounds c1960 T114017

Tilbury's very name implies that there has always been a fortification here. Tilbury Fort, as we know it, was originally built by Henry VIII and remodelled under later monarchs. Elizabeth I was staying here when she learnt of the Armada's defeat. The picture shows part of the star-shaped moat built by Charles II's chief engineer.

▲ Chadwell St Mary
Chadwell Place c1955

C239005

Chadwell - meaning 'cold well' - occupies a ridge of high ground above the Thames. Chadwell Place now sits a few hundred yards off the busy Chadwell Bypass, though it still manages to hold its own. Apart from the presence of a grain silo peering over its shoulder, the cream-painted farmhouse seems unchanged since the 1950s.

◄ **Chadwell St Mary River View c1960** C239013 This parade of shops appeared between the wars, when Chadwell started stretching out along the road to Grays. In 1960 the row included Harvey's newsagents, Achille Serre cleaners, and Colwell's hairdressing. Nowadays there is a florist, a charity shop and a trailer shop. As the street name suggests, there are views into Kent from here.

◀ **Orsett**
High Street c1960 044001

Orsett is a compact village
built on a grid of streets.
Before the industrialisation
of Grays and Tilbury, Orsett
was a kind of administrative
centre for the area. It was
bypassed by the railway and
from then on its importance
declined. The village church
is set back from the road,
behind the trees on the left.

Chadwell St Mary
Defoe Parade c1960

C239012

The Parade's name is not arbitrary; Daniel Defoe lived in Chadwell in the 1690s, and opened a tile factory in the parish. The business failed, and he lost £3,000 - a result, he said, of being imprisoned for writing a controversial religious pamphlet. One likes to think his sense of enterprise lived on, though, in VG Foodmarket and neighbours.

Orsett
Larkins Corner c1960

044010

Larkins Corner, allegedly the oldest house in Orsett, is a 15th-century structure, named after a former tenant. It is partly pargetted (has ornamental plasterwork on the outside). Prince Charles Avenue was previously called Hall Road. It led to Orsett Hall, which was sold in 1974 and subsequently became a restaurant.

Orsett
Whitmore Arms and
Birch Cottages c1960

044006

Once known as the George, the Whitmore Arms takes its name from Sir Francis Whitmore, Lord Lieutenant of Essex, who lived at Orsett Hall. When he died in 1962, the pub sign was draped in black. Between the building's upper windows are the family's two crests, which are a hawk on a tree stump, and an arm between two wings.

◀ **Horndon-on-the-Hill High Street c1960**

H178006

Horndon's Woolmarket, where trading took place, is the weatherboarded building behind the lorry. The Bell, opposite, was an important coaching inn, and still has a high reputation today. It dates from the 15th century. The bell on the sign bears the motto 'I call for the living, I toll for the dead, I scatter the lightning'.

Horndon-on-the-Hill
View from the Hill
c1960 H178008
As its name suggests, Horndon occupies an eminence overlooking the Thames. The refineries at Shell Haven and Coryton can be seen in the distance. These fields once provided grazing for the sheep on which Horndon's early prosperity was founded. It was a market town specialising in wool, although its status dwindled after the flocks declined in the 16th century.

Horndon-on-the-Hill
High Street c1960 H178001
This view is looking north; the houses nearest us were once commercial premises, consisting of a hardware store and a tailor. To the rear of them lies Swan Meadow, once home to the village fair. This event survives as Horndon-on-the-Hill Feast & Fayre, which takes place each year at the end of June, to mark St Peter's Day.

Mucking
The Church c1960 M386043
Mucking is scarcely a village at all these days. The church is down a dead-end road, which is used only by sand and ballast lorries. The final christening was held here in 1981. It was later converted into a house, and its graveyard is now inaccessible. Nearby, the school-cum-village-hall is now disused, and the Crown public house is an office.

◄ **Stanford-le-Hope
The Pavement c1955**

S258306

In this view, bicycles still rule the road. Stanford's Pavement had previously consisted of a row of weatherboarded houses. By the 1950s, there was Hart's butcher's shop, Arnold's hairdressers (note the stripy pole and the signs for Brylcreem, as well as the 'male-interest' tobacco ads), Searle's grocer's shop, and Eade the greengrocer's.

◀ Stanford-le-Hope
The Station c1960

S258060
The 'Hope' in Stanford-le-Hope is the name of a bend in the Thames. The railway arrived here in 1855. Like neighbouring Corringham, Stanford was used to house workers from the Kynochtown explosives factory, and later from nearby oil refineries. New housing is being built in the background of this photograph.

▼ Stanford-le-Hope
Camping Ground
c1955 S258310
On Mucking Creek, south of Stanford, there used to be a wharf; hence the name of Wharf Road. This area, Stanford Marshes, accommodates a variety of wildlife, and there is a bird sanctuary stretching down to Mucking. Gravel was once excavated here, though the pits are now used for sailing.

◀ Stanford-le-Hope
The Green c1960

S258007
This is still Stanford's central point, but 'The Green' has long been something of a misnomer. Here we see, to the right of the war memorial, Chapman's Quality Foods, which is now part florist, part opticians. Dominating the parade, with its placard for Dunlop Rubber Boots, is Ager's Complete Outfitters, which is now a hair salon.

Stanford-le-Hope
The War Memorial c1960 S258061
Barclay's Bank is now an antique-centre-cum-pawnbroker: is this a sign of the times? The right hand part of the bank was formerly home to S Cowell, ironmonger. Lloyd's Bank was built on the site of the Cock & Magpie, which was once a smugglers' pub. It was three hundred years old when demolished in 1929.

Stanford-le-Hope
Looking North East c1960 S258027
This is a vista from the tower of St Margaret's church. Note how there are very few cars about. The dominant building (centre left) is the Methodist church. Three doors to the right is a shop with a plaque on the side: it is a shoe advert, which reads 'Just Right! Made by John White, Stocked by Graylin's.' (It is still there.)

Corringham
Bull Inn c1955 C243005
Corringham still retains some old buildings. The Bull dates largely from the 17th century, though the wing on the right, with its projecting gable, is two centuries older. Like so many pubs around here, it has smuggling associations: it is riddled with sliding panels, double doors and secret chambers. A weekly animal market used to be held outside.

◄ **Corringham**
Shell Haven Refinery
c1967 C243571
Although the oil refinery is now owned by Shell, the name Shell Haven was already occurring on maps four hundred years ago. It simply indicated that part of the estuary where tidal currents deposited a large number of shells (these were used for making mortar). Oil was first stored here in 1912 by the Asiatic Petroleum Company.

Corringham
Woodbrooke Way c1955 C243044
These shops serve an outlying part of Corringham. They are the usual
mix of grocer, hardware shop and newsagent, the latter with a weighing-
machine outside. The lady is still using a large coach-built pram, which
was soon to be superseded by collapsible buggies like the one to her
left. The car is an early Morris Minor with a divided windscreen.

Corringham, Lampits Hill c1950 C243014
Corringham was a small, remote village before the coming of the oil refineries; the Shell sign in the distance says it all. This parade was built in 1929. The two delivery vans are of different vintages, the smaller being a pre-War model, whilst the box-van is somewhat later.

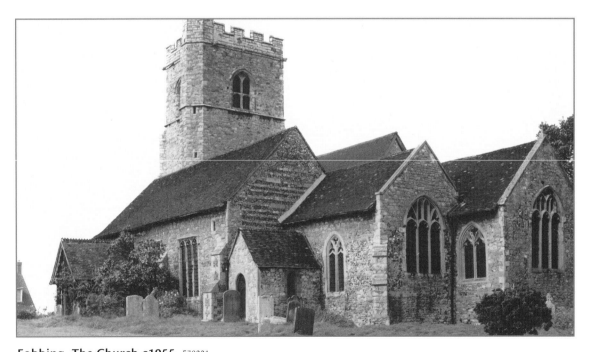

Fobbing, The Church c1955 F78001
The grey ragstone tower of St Michael's overlooks Shell Haven. The turret's spiral staircase contains about a hundred steps. Smuggling once took place at Fobbing Creek, which used to be more navigable than it is now, and one can imagine the church being a useful landmark. A beacon by night, even.

**Canvey Island
Thorney Bay Beach
Camp c1955** C237304
Thorney Bay has a
surprisingly sandy
beach. The holiday
village started life as a
campsite. By the 1950s
its amenities included a
café, an open-air theatre,
and a reception building.
There was also a boating
pool, which was popular
with locals and visitors,
and a number of kiosks
selling ice cream and
buckets and spades.

Canvey Island Beach c1950 C237004
"A week in Canvey will do you more good than a fortnight elsewhere", ran an early slogan. By the 1920s, up to 50,000 day trippers were visiting the island on a bank holiday, and it was still a popular destination when this photo was taken. Canvey had initially been marketed as a holiday haven for East Londoners.

Canvey Island
Beach House Restaurant c1955 C237122
The Beach House Restaurant has now gone. Its main clientele were
the boating fraternity, and residents of the surrounding caravan
park. This picture shows Canvey's flat terrain, much of which is
below the level of the spring tides. Large tracts of the island were
reclaimed from the sea by Dutch engineers in the 17th century.

Canvey Island, Beach c1955 C237065
Pleasure-boat trips were among Canvey's first attractions. Here, the motor launch 'Summer Rose' is offering 'long sea trips' (with, below, the cryptic injunction 'Do not proceed beyond line of saplings'). Notice that there are no shadows, and that, other than the boy in the foreground, nobody is really dressed for the beach.

South Benfleet, The Parade c1955 S278032
These days Hopes Green is simply a westward extension of South Benfleet, but it started life as a hamlet of fishermen's cottages. In fact, a navigable creek once brought boats right up to where we are standing, which is near the entrance to the playing fields. What would the fishermen have made of shops such as Dressywear?

◀ **South Benfleet
The Creek c1960**

S278054

Not so long ago, Benfleet was principally geared up to fishing. There had also once been a timber trade here, as the slopes were heavily wooded. The bridge in the picture connects Canvey Island to the mainland. Prior to 1931, there had only been a causeway (covered at high tide) and a ferryman, made redundant by the bridge.

South Benfleet
The Anchor c1960
S278064

The building that later became the Anchor was first erected in 1380. Evidently it was a well-liked place, since a song was published about it in 1918: "There's good entertainment for man and beast / At this ancient smuggler's nest ...". At that time, Benfleet's only public transport, a horse and carriage, operated from outside the pub.

Thundersley
View from Churchyard c1955
T113027

St Peter's church squats in an imposing position above a terraced graveyard. Further westwards are the extensive dormitories of New Thundersley and Tarpots, joining onto Benfleet. Presumably Thundersley's hill was a pagan site, as the parish's name means 'clearing dedicated to Thunor', a Saxon god of thunder.

Hadleigh
The Castle 1891 29071

Hadleigh Castle was built in 1232 by Hubert de Burgh, the Chief Justiciar. A man of lowly birth, he was effectively the regent during Henry III's childhood. The castle's curtain wall enclosed one acre of land. A later owner, Lord Rich of Leighs, had it partly demolished in the 16th century for building materials.

▼ **Hadleigh**

The Castle 1891 29069

The Castle had long been a romantic ruin, overrun with ivy and brushwood, when Constable painted it. It was already "much resorted to in summer by picnic parties", said a guidebook. The four corner towers, of which only two survive to any great height, have walls 9 ft thick at the base.

▼ **Hadleigh**

Looking East c1950 H167005

One of the problems faced by Hadleigh Castle was the risk of landslides on the slopes overlooking the Thames. They demolished as much of the walls as any unscrupulous owner could. In 1891, General Booth acquired some land here, and it became the Salvation Army's first colony. It was a farm where skills could be taught to the destitute.

▲ **Hadleigh**

High Street c1950

H167010

The old High Street had been bypassed by the 1920s, hence its tranquil air. The white building behind the trees is Hadleigh Hall, a 19th-century rebuilding of an earlier "mansion". It was dismantled in 1961. The pub in the foreground started life as the Boar's Head, before becoming the Blue Boar, and then the Castle.

◀ **Hadleigh**

Kingsway c1950 H16/012
The Kingsway Cinema
opened in 1936 with a film
called 'Jack Of All Trades'.
It survived until the early
70s, when it made way for a
supermarket. On the corner
is Arthur Yeaxlee's drapery
shop. Originally in the
High Street, he moved to
Kingsway, the new bypass,
to take advantage of the
re-routed traffic. Yeaxlee's
sold-up in 1967.

◄ **Hadleigh
High Street c1960**

H167014

Back in the old High Street, life went on. An Esso garage had replaced the humble pumps in the earlier photograph. The lane in the foreground, on the left, is Endway, which was once home to Hadleigh's best-known resident, the witch doctor Cunning Murrell. Part alchemist, part faith healer, he died in 1860 and was buried in Hadleigh churchyard.

Hadleigh
Central Parade c1950

H167003

Since the 1890s, there had been clamour for traffic improvements in Hadleigh. Built on land owned by the Salvation Army and Wells & Perry's brewery, the bypass finally opened in 1924. These shops (one of which is sporting a pleasantly chocoholic advert) soon sprang up along it. The trees conceal the historic church of St James the Less.

Hadleigh
London Road c1960

H167015

Compare this with the view of the High Street in 1950. We are at the top of that road, looking at where Hadleigh Hall had stood. It is hard to imagine now, but there were once some tea gardens behind the house in the foreground. By the 1950s there was evidently some kind of hardware enterprise taking place here instead.

Leigh-on-Sea
From the West 1891

29065

Before being absorbed by Southend, Leigh was a fishing village specialising in cockles, winkles, shrimps, oysters and whitebait. The spoil-heaps seen here on the beach are, indeed, cockles. There is still a fishing trade here, supplying the local cafés and pubs. Up the hill, the 80 ft tower of St Clement's church pokes above the trees.

▼ **Leigh-on-Sea**
High Street c1950 L30024
When the railway came to Leigh, it virtually touched the High Street, The original station stood in the space on the right. The building immediately behind the telegraph pole had been built by a mariner in 1589. Later Jack Juniper's fish shop, it was pulled down in 1952. Tradition claims that Constable lodged there while painting Hadleigh Castle.

▼ **Leigh-on-Sea**
Cliff Shelter c1955 L30039
"Leigh-on-Sea does not present a particularly clean appearance", said a Southend guidebook of 1901. Nevertheless, it was incorporated into the borough in 1914, and its undercliff now represents one of Southend's less raucous pleasures. But it is a far cry from the days when the old High Street was the only built-up part of Leigh.

▲ **Southend-on-Sea**
Royal Terrace 1891
29061
New South-End was a would-be fashionable resort that, by the turn of the 19th century, was struggling. Then, in 1803, Princess Caroline came to stay at The Terrace. Since the Princess did not enjoy an unsullied reputation, one might imagine such patronage to have been harmful. Not so; Southend suddenly took off, and The Terrace became 'Royal Terrace'.

◀ **Southend-on-Sea
From the Pier 1898**
41379
During the 19th century, the town mushroomed. "You could not have a softer climate or sunnier skies than this much abused Southend," wrote Disraeli in 1833. The area west of the pier, seen here, was always regarded as the 'nicer' part of Southend. Royal Terrace, with its wrought-iron balconies, is perched on the cliff top.

**Southend-on-Sea
The Beach 1898** 40912
The bathing machine
was a mid-19th-century
innovation designed to
protect the modesty
of female bathers. The
machines glossed over
the awkward processes
of getting changed
and into the water,
which was particularly
necessary at a time
when most men swam
nude. The Southend
machines' proprietor,
Harry Absalom, later
invented a type of
floating swimming pool.

Southend-on-Sea
The Esplanade 1898

41384

"The New Covered Seats on the Esplanade are a grand improvement. Visitors cannot fail to realise this", said an early guidebook. This photo tells us much about a Victorian beach - umbrellas used as parasols, sailor suits for boys, nannies in white pinafores, hats everywhere, skiffs for hire. The bathing costume, as such, does not really exist.

**Southend-on-Sea
Boating Beach
c1950** S155018
The stretch of seafront
east of the pier is
referred to as the
Golden Mile. It includes
the Kursaal, a large
domed building, built
in 1901, with attached
pleasure grounds. This
was an idea inspired
by Blackpool's Winter
Gardens. It contained a
menagerie, a ballroom,
a funfair, a cycling track,
and much more. The
name means 'cure-all'.

Southend-on-Sea
From the Pier 1898 40910
The pier's ornate brick frontage dates
from 1885; it was dismantled in the
1930s. Behind it, the Royal Hotel occupies
the eastern end of Royal Terrace. The
Terrace also housed Southend's original
assembly room. This part of the front is
now an area of imported sand.

Southend-on-Sea
The Golden Hind c1955 S155040
Southend is not where one might expect
to find Drake's famous ship. In fact, this
is a full-sized replica, built in 1949 by
twelve local mariners. Madame Tussaud's
provided wax figures of Sir Francis and his
crew. In recent years, it has been replaced
by another facsimile ship, Blackbeard's
'Queen Anne's Revenge'.

Southend-on-Sea
Palace Hotel and Beach c1955 S155001
The Palace Hotel dominates Southend. Originally to be called the
Metropole, it was built on the site of a fairground (which was allegedly
"a hideous contrivance" in any case). It finally opened as the Palace at
Whitsun 1904. During the Great War, it served a very different purpose,
as it became the Queen Mary Royal Naval Hospital.

▼ **Southend-on-Sea**

The Pier 1947 S155009

Southend has the longest pleasure pier in the world. An earlier pier, made entirely of wood, was in place by 1830. In 1889 it made way for an iron structure, which with various alterations and extensions, is the pier we see today. The Pavilion (with cupola) was destroyed by a fire in 1959.

▼ **Southend-on-Sea**

The Pier c1955 S155070

Note the sign saying 'Trains To Pier Head': these were electric trains that ran people and luggage to steamers and pier-head restaurants. They were installed in 1890. To the left is the children's boating lake. Though it was well loved in its day, it was drained in the 1970s and the Adventure Island funfair now occupies its site.

▲ **Southend-on-Sea**
Aerial View c1955

S155044

This is a fascinating view. The area in the foreground was built in 1918 as the Sunken Gardens, though later, as Peter Pan's Playground, it included a speedway and a small zoo. The Palace Hotel is by far the biggest building, while to the east, the front is a string of amusements and fast-food outlets.

◀ **Southend-on-Sea The Beach c1960** S155133
This is a strangely ancient looking view of Southend. This is probably due to the presence of the Shrubbery, a patch of woodland that was spared when New South-End was originally mapped out in the 1790s. It became popular in itself as a venue for entertainments, and now includes 'Never Never Land'.

▼ Prittlewell
The Church 1891 29075

Prittlewell's name means 'babbling spring', which supposedly referred to a well at the nearby Cluniac priory. According to the Domesday Book, there was already a church of some importance here before the Conquest - and the current structure contains what seems to be a 7th-century doorway. This was the mother parish of Southend, which was, quite simply, the 'south end' of Prittlewell.

▼ Shoeburyness
The Garrison Clock-Tower c1955 S275006

The cornerstones of Shoeburyness are brickworks, railways, farming, and the military. The Royal Artillery Garrison and School Of Gunnery first came here in the mid 19th century. Although the last regiment served here in 1975, a limited presence was maintained until 1998. Soldiers here would often remain in the town with their families, after retirement.

▲ **Shoeburyness Rampart Terrace c1955** S275043
The name 'Shoeburyness' means 'encampment on the shoe-shaped piece of land'. The earthwork in question was thrown up in 894 by Haesten, a "lusty and terrifying" Danish chieftain who had just been routed at Benfleet by King Alfred. The sea and the barracks have obliterated most of it, though Rampart Street marks its northeast side.

◀ Shoeburyness
The Promenade c1955

S275016

During the depression of the 1930s, in order to combat local unemployment, efforts were made to turn Shoeburyness into a tourist resort. It was "one of the healthiest resorts in England". Holidaymakers are still welcomed here today: there are still beach-huts and a café, though other features such as a putting green and a boating lake have gone.

◄ **Shoeburyness
East Beach c1960** S275069
In the 19th century, there
were brickfields and a smithy
on the beach, but by the
1930s they were gone, and
there were reputedly 600
deckchairs for hire instead.
A fair number are available
in this scene, too, though
business does not appear
to be brisk. Nevertheless,
it is worth noting that
Shoeburyness is officially the
driest corner of England.

**Shoeburyness
Shoebury Hall Farm
Camp c1955** S275026
The concept of the
caravan park was born
in the post-War years.
This particular one was
especially popular with
Londoners. When it closed
in 1974, there were 375
caravans and a shop on
the site. The camp was
known for its 'select'
standards and friendly
atmosphere. There is
housing here now.

▼ **Shoeburyness
East Beach Tent Site
c1960** S275095
East Beach remains
popular, as it is handy for
the station and has a café,
a car park, and a large
grassy play area. In the
1930s, there had been
plans to lay out a high-
class holiday estate here,
but the cold winds and
the military atmosphere
(not to mention the noise
of the ordnance), were
not really conducive to
the idea.

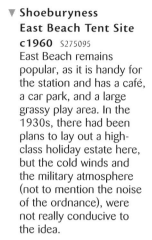

◄ **Little Wakering
Village c1965** L559023
Little Wakering
comprises one long
street, now continuous
with the neighbouring
villages of Barling and
Great Wakering. The
tower of St Mary's
church, which can be
seen in the distance
with its slightly crooked
spire, was donated by
John Wakering. He was a
15th-century Bishop of
Norwich. Several of the
adjacent offshore islands
used to be included in
this parish.

◄ **Rochford**
The Golf Links c1955

R226021

With only Rochford Hall and a golf course for company, St Andrew's church is an imposing building. It is well known for its late 15th-century redbrick tower and the half-timbered Tudor gables (complete with chimney) on the north side. The Hall, just to our right, was once the residence of the Boleyn family, including Anne.

Rochford
North Street c1955

R226003

Rochford stands on the river to which it gives its name - the Roach. Four ancient roads cross here, and there is a square that was granted a market in 1257. There are still some old weatherboarded houses to be seen, though some of those pictured here have gone. The post office was once the town's police station.

Rochford
Market Place c1965

R226039

The Maypole Self Service store projects onto the Square on the site of the former Market House. Built in 1707, early photos show this as a decrepit-looking timber structure with a bellcote. It housed pigs, the town's fire engine and a barber's shop, and had a room upstairs for weighing wool. It was demolished in 1861.

Rochford Stambridge Mill

c1955 R226011

These mill workers were part of a very long established business: there was already a mill at Stambridge when the Domesday Book was compiled. Once jokingly dubbed Rochford-on-Sea (but properly called Palm Beach), this spot has always been popular with locals. It is famous for the purple carpet of sea lavender that blooms here.

▼ Paglesham

The Stores c1955 P143002

Paglesham, on the River Roach, has two distinct 'ends', Eastend and Churchend. Here we see Eastend Post Office, which was built in 1873 by James Wiseman, a local oyster magnate. The cottages on the right, Barn Row, were constructed at the same time; they are now a holiday home. The shop closed in 1985 and became a house.

▼ Paglesham

The River Roach c1955 P143004

While much of Paglesham's livelihood derived from oysters, it was also an agricultural parish. Essex barges, like this one, were called 'stackies' when stacked up with hay for the London market (where it was sold as horse-fodder). They would race each other up the Thames, laying their masts horizontally when passing under bridges.

▲ Wallasea Bay
The Jetty c1955

W187001

Wallasea is one of six very flat islands in what is called the Essex Archipelago. This expectant crowd are awaiting the ferry to Burnham, on the opposite side of the Crouch. Apart from a timber yard, a large caravan park, a pub, and the ever-expanding Essex Yacht Marina, Wallasea is practically empty.

◀ **Canewdon
High Street c1965** C236002
Canewdon is a small village on the south bank of the River Crouch. The pub seen here, the Anchor, is where the parish vestry used to meet. Outside the village is an earthwork where Canute encamped his army prior to the nearby Battle of Ashingdon (which he won), although Canewdon's name is not derived from the King's.

**Burnham-on-Crouch
High Street c1960**

B325032

Burnham's High Street does not run straight, but follows a curve parallel to the River Crouch. Quite rightly, too, for the river is Burnham's reason for existence. It was the first firm landing place for vessels sailing up the estuary. The High Street's width reminds us that it was once a medieval marketplace. Now much of it is a Conservation Area.

◄ **Burnham-on-Crouch
The Quay c1960**

B325034

The coastguards' tower, the marine stores, the crane and the paddling children all indicate Burnham's many faces. The town is now a major yachting centre; the large white building in the distance is the home of the Royal Corinthian Yacht Club. It was built in 1931 in Art Deco style, and it won an architectural award.

◄ Burnham-on-Crouch High Street c1950

B325005

The most conspicuous feature here is the Clock Tower. It was built in 1877, in memory of Laban Sweeting, an oyster merchant who had done much for the town. On the day of his funeral, all the shops closed out of respect. Also involved with oysters were the Auger family, who erected Warners Hall, the tall house in the middle-distance.

▼ Burnham-on-Crouch Town Steps c1965 B325107

This photograph shows a sunny day on the Crouch. Although much of Burnham's revenue came from oysters and boat building, it was also an important wool port in the heyday of East Anglia's wool trade. The buildings along the Quay still have a stateliness about them, and are painted in a variety of colours.

◄ Southminster High Street c1955 S279001

This is a quiet day in Southminster, one of the larger villages of the Dengie peninsula. Indeed, it once had no fewer than 15 pubs. The High Street only became the centre of the village's shopping activity after the Second World War, as a bomb had devastated the previous main shopping thoroughfare, North Street.

▼ **Southminster**

Hall Road and the Old Pump c1955 S279003
The Bishops of London, who owned Southminster, donated this pump in 1831. To the left is the edge of Pandole Wood, which the Elizabethans used as a rubbish dump, and the Victorians as a picnic site. Although this road junction is now four miles from the coast, the sea once came right up to the edge of the wood.

▼ **Tillingham**

The Square c1955 T115026
After Tillingham's green became criss-crossed by roads, it became known as The Square. Once surrounded by shops, it now makes do with visits from mobile vans, such as a library, a butcher, and a fish & chip van. There was a strong temperance movement here in the 19th century, which the Fox & Hounds was lucky to survive. Other pubs did not.

▲ **Bradwell-on-Sea
The Quay c1960**

B177001
Standing at the very mouth of the Blackwater estuary, this rough wooden wharf was once a significant quay for the surrounding area. Before railways and lorries, it was the best means of transporting farm produce. Hay would be shipped from here, while incoming cargoes might include London sewage for mucking the fields, or Kentish ragstone for facing the sea walls.

◀ **Bradwell-on-Sea Chapel of St Peter-on-the-Wall c1960** B177002
St Peter's was established by St Cedd, a Northumbrian missionary faced with reintroducing Christianity into southern Britain. It dates from the 650s, and has survived various alternative uses, which included a lighthouse and a barn, as you can see by the bricked-up doorway, which was big enough for a hay cart. The 'Wall' in the name refers to the foundations of Othona, a Roman fort.

◀ **St Lawrence
The Stone c1955**

S825015

So good, they named it four times, this small settlement on the southern shore of the Blackwater estuary, is variously known as Ramsey Island, St Lawrence Bay, Steeple Stone, and just The Stone. Before the 1890s, it only consisted of Wick Farm, and a muddy lane that is now the village's Main Road.

◄ **Bradwell-on-Sea**
St Thomas's Church
c1955 B177011
Bradwell is a scattered community. The centre, two miles from the sea, is clustered around St Thomas's church with its 18th-century redbrick tower. The building with the projecting bracket is the King's Head, which has always been something of a social centre, and used as a meeting place by several groups.

▼ **St Lawrence**
The Stone, The Yacht Club and Oyster Cottages
c1955 S825028
By 1902, a Mr Winterbon and a Mr Cauldwell had built eight two-up-two-down cottages, the Oyster Cottages, just behind the sea wall. The following year, the Riverview Guest House sprang up beside them. It later became the Stone Yacht Club. The man seen here outside the cottages is using an early model of rotary mower, called a Rotoscythe.

◄ **St Lawrence**
The Stone, Waterfront
c1955 S825041
After the Second World War, the Riverview Guest House had become a yacht club in order to gain a licence, though it engaged in little yachting. Nevertheless, its refreshments had always been popular with sailing types. Despite changes at The Stone, fishing has never entirely died out: note the 'cockles, shrimps, mussels' available at the shack.

◄ **Osea Island**
Osea Farm 1903 50234
One man and his chickens
stroll through Osea, a low-
lying island of 243 acres
in the Blackwater estuary.
It is now entirely in private
ownership, and includes
a farm (see the barn on
the left). There was once
a general store (right) with
a post box saying that the
next collection would be
'according to the tide'.

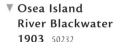

**◄ St Lawrence
The Stone c1955**

S825018

Because of a post-War recession in the shipping industry, the Blackwater at this point was used to 'lay up' unwanted cargo ships. Some of them were quite large, and the photo may well show one of them. Otherwise, the boats here are pleasure craft. The Stone's main draws now are water-skiing, jet-skiing and windsurfing.

**▼ Osea Island
River Blackwater
1903** 50232

Osea is the closest boats can be taken to Maldon and remain floating at all stages of the tide. Barges often stopped here to unload into smaller vessels. A drying-out home for inebriates was once installed on Osea. That the plan failed was due, in part, to local boatmen smuggling alcohol onto the island, naturally for a fee.

**◄ Maldon
The Hythe 1891** 29077

At the time of this photo, Maldon had a healthy shipping trade in corn, coal, chalk and hay. The Hythe itself (a word meaning 'landing-place') was full of maltings, flourmills, ropewalks and boatyards. This view has not changed much, although, to the left, a large Marine Lake was opened in 1905.

▼ **Maldon**
The Hythe c1960 M12103
Maldon is still popular with boating enthusiasts, some of whom
preserve a handful of the old brown-sailed barges. A mile behind
where the photographer is standing is the site of Maldon's claim to
historical fame; its Battle of 991, and the eponymous Anglo-Saxon
poem that describes the event. To cut a long story short, we lost.

▼ **Heybridge**
The Square c1955 H174018
The Square's name belies its shape, as it is now a roundabout. The
Half Moon opened as licensed premises in 1769. Evidently this was a
sporting pub, as it once had a skittle-alley, and was the headquarters of
Heybridge Cricket Club. Perhaps these cyclists used it too. The other
vehicle in our picture appears to be a motorised invalid-carriage.

▲ **Heybridge
Bathing from the
Quarter Deck Café
c1960** H174312
Heybridge Basin is where
the Chelmer & Blackwater
Navigation joins the
actual Blackwater
estuary. The waterfront
is a popular spot with
day-trippers and native
'Basiners', boating people
and swimmers. The girl
in the middle has all the
accessories: the bathing
cap and the hastily
inflated rubber ring.

◀ **Heybridge Yacht Store and Quarter Deck Café c1960** H174309
The Basin Yacht Store offered 'Yachts, Mooring, Maintenance, Calor Gas, Winter Storage, Marine Paints, Clothing etc'. This photo says a lot about traditional British holidaymakers, making do with a length of sea wall, some scrubby grass and concrete steps, and not afraid to wear their carpet slippers at the seafront!

**Tollesbury
Looking North-West
c1955** T117051
The church tower
commands a fine view
of this big village on
the marshes. As it is a
relatively out-of-the-way
place, the buses were
a lifeline. The ones here
are Osborne's buses,
named after George,
a carrier who saw the
potential of automobiles
early on. The company
kept going until 1997.

▼ Tollesbury

Woodrolfe Creek c1955 T117040

Woodrolfe (pronounced 'Woodrope') is a world of boatyards and slipways. Oysters used to be raised here. Among the buildings in the background are Tollesbury's famous yacht stores, where craft were housed out-of-season. Yachting is still important here, and there is now a marina in the vicinity.

▼ East Mersea

Coopers Beach c1960 E68303

Mersea is a large offshore island, measuring 4½ miles by 2. It is divided into two parishes, East and West. The latter has always been the more commercialised, but East Mersea, too, has clusters of chalets and caravans around its shingly beaches. The folklorist and hymn-writer Sabine Baring-Gould (famous for 'Onward Christian Soldiers') was rector here in the 1870s.

▲ Wivenhoe
The Quay and River c1955 W160008

Wivenhoe used to serve as the outer port of Colchester, as vessels too large to reach Colchester Hythe would discharge here. Shipbuilding took place here too, though both shipyard and port are now closed. In their heyday, the town's shipwrights produced a man-of-war for Cromwell's navy.

◄ **Wivenhoe**
The River c1955 W160007
This is a view of Wivenhoe's slipway, and some of its attractive riverfront houses. Across the Colne lies the smaller quay of Fingringhoe, connected by a recently reinstated ferry. These days, according to the poet Martin Newell, Wivenhoe is "part suburbia, part bohemia / with a dash of academia": it is noted for its mix of social types.

◀ **Brightlingsea
Jacobs c1955** B209024
Jacobs was the home of the
Beriffes, a family of wealthy
shipping merchants, who
bought it in about 1400.
It had taken its name from
earlier owners. The curious
stair-turret was added in the
15th century, presumably
to save the space an inside
staircase would take up. By
the 1950s, Jacobs was a
café offering 'Coffee, Tea,
Ices'.

◄ **Brightlingsea Anchor Hotel 1907**

57564

Brightlingsea has always been a seagoing community, as the Anchor's name reminds us. So, too, does the ensign on the flagpole. Standing by the foreshore, the hotel had opened only two years before this picture was taken. It replaced an earlier weatherboarded structure. The implement parked in front seems to be some kind of seed-drill.

**Brightlingsea ►
Parish Church c1955**

B209028

All Saints' occupies a ridge one mile from the town. Its flint tower, 94 ft high, is an important seamark. One 19th-century vicar, the Rev Arthur Pertwee, used to stand on the parapet with a lantern, hoping to guide seafarers home. Inside the church, any townspeople lost at sea are commemorated with a special plaque. This was Pertwee's idea.

◄ **St Osyth
The Priory 1895** 35698

Previously known as Chich, the village of St Osyth takes its name from an East Anglian princess. She established a nunnery here, though in 653 it was sacked by Danes and Osyth was beheaded. A holy well gushed forth where her head hit the ground. St Osyth Priory, founded in 1118, supposedly occupies the nunnery's site.

◄ **Jaywick**
Martello Tower Holiday
Camp c1955 J4021
This view shows an odd
combination of ancient and
modern. Jaywick is flanked
by a pair of Martello towers.
One of them, seen here
on the right, overlooks
a caravan park. These
towers were inspired by a
fortification at Mortella Point
in Corsica. Impressed by its
impregnability, the British
threw up a string of them as
coastal defences during the
Napoleonic Wars.

◄ **Jaywick
Brooklands c1955**

J4041

This is Essex's archetypal seaside development. The fields that became Jaywick were originally sold after the agricultural depression of the late 1920s. The land was divided into plots, and wooden chalets erected on them. In 1930 the first went up for sale for £50. Initially, these were only intended as holiday homes.

▼ **Jaywick
The Sea Wall c1955** J4036

This picture encapsulates several of Jaywick's charms, The building with the jauntily curved roofline is the Playdium, a casino and an amusement arcade. The Savoy, advertising table-tennis, was likewise an amusement centre. Fish and chips are also on offer. Note how heavily defended the front is: Jaywick has always taken a hammering from the sea.

◄ **Jaywick
The Promenade and Sea Wall c1955** J4052

By the time this photo was taken, Jaywick had become a popular small resort. The whole town had an informal feel, like a holiday camp, as the facia of The Cabin suggests: 'Gifts - Sweets - Films - Ice-Cream'. The local authorities had initially been reluctant to recognise Jaywick, claiming its marshy land was unsuited to development.

▼ **Jaywick**

Brooklands c1955 J4033

This is a good study of some typical Jaywick chalets. The town was cheery enough in holiday weather, but things were not always so 'hi-de-hi'. In 1953, just beyond where the trio are cavorting on the 'Jaywick Socials' tricycle, the sea had smashed a thirty-yard gap in the concrete sea wall. This resulted in the town flooding, leaving 35 people dead.

▼ **Jaywick**

The Sands c1955 J4037

One of Jaywick's many quirks is that all the roads on its Brooklands estate are named after makes of car, such as Buick Avenue, Wolseley Avenue, and Hillman Avenue. Some of them, not unlike the town itself, now have a pleasantly nostalgic ring to them. The picture illustrates a mode of transport more intimately connected with the seaside.

▲ **Jaywick, The Sands**
c1955 J4038
This is a quintessential 1950s beach scene: beach balls are being clutched, children are digging, and men are cultivating quiffs. With the tide out, Jaywick Sands are surprisingly expansive in both length and breadth. On the horizon is the second of Jaywick's two Martello towers. Beyond lies Butlin's and Clacton-on-Sea.

◄ **Great Clacton
The Yew Trees 1913**

65244

Great Clacton was the mother parish of Clacton-on-Sea. This view sees us looking westwards along The Street, now St John's Road, towards the big Norman church of St John the Baptist. The buildings on the extreme right included the Queen's Head; and a row of shops, which were demolished in the 1960s.

▲ **Clacton-on-Sea**
From the Pier 1891 28227
Until 1864, Clacton had simply been a row of
cliffs. It was Peter Bruff, a railway engineer,
who bought the land and started to develop a
resort here. It was certainly attracting visitors
by 1891, albeit well covered ones. Perhaps
it was winter. On the left is a Martello tower,
which acted as a coastguard station.

Clacton-on-Sea ▶
Pier Avenue 1891 28230
Pier Avenue had something of a Wild West
appearance, a notion reinforced by the
advert for 'American iced drinks'. Down the
road, where the sign says 'Carriages', the
Criterion Hotel offered "landaus, wagonettes,
broughams ... on hire at most reasonable
charges." It also boasted "accommodation for
tricycles", among other things.

Clacton-on-Sea
The Pier 1901 46692
The pier, which dates
from 1871, swarms
with black - clad
holidaymakers. A fleet
of steamers plied to
and from the pier-head.
The timetable on the
Ladies' Baths advertises
services to Felixstowe,
Harwich, Ipswich,
Yarmouth, Southend and
Gravesend. A camera
obscura and a Pavilion
also graced the pier.

Clacton-on-Sea
The Town Hall 1904 51538
The majestic Town Hall, built 1894, comprised a Barclay's Bank
downstairs, council offices upstairs, and an Operetta House at the
back. It was badly damaged in May 1941 by a bomb, which also
destroyed the opposite corner. Nine years later, Barclay's was
rebuilt on the same site, with a slightly more modest clock tower.
It is still there today.

Clacton-on-Sea

Bridge and Pier 1921 70264 with detail left
The Venetian Bridge had replaced a row of
gift-stalls and "winkle and eel-pie shops",
that had been shut down before the Great
War due to unsanitary conditions. In 1921,
the pier had just been acquired by the
Kingsman family, who were to own it for
nearly 50 years. The White Coons were a
popular troupe here between the wars.

**Clacton-on-Sea
Band Pavilion 1914**

66847
Dating from 1899, Clacton's bandstand had recently been relocated to this new sunken pavilion as part of a "general beautifying programme". The picture was taken in that long hot summer before the declaration of war. Everyone is wearing a hat, the women's wide-brimmed, rounded style being typical of the period. Electric lighting was installed on the prom in 1912.

▼ **Holland-on-Sea**
The View from the Cliffs c1955 H177051
Before 1900, Little Holland was a sparsely populated farming parish
with a ruined medieval church. Then, 250 acres of cliff top land were
auctioned, and plans drawn up for a new resort. As late as the 1920s,
it still clung onto some of its old rural self. A decade later it had
become what we now call Holland-on-Sea.

▼ **Holland-on-Sea**
Kings Avenue c1945 H177001
The Queen's Hall, built in the 1930s, was an important part of Holland's
social scene. It had a café, tea gardens and a luncheon & tea room.
There was a theatre in the hall, and the fine parquet floor was ideal for
old-time dancing. A badminton club was established here in the 1940s.
There are now flats on the site.

▲ **Holland-on-Sea**
The Roaring Donkey
c1945 H177003
Pub names such as
the 'Goat In Boots' or
the 'Roaring Donkey'
were generally mocking
references to Napoleon.
This particular Donkey,
though, did not exist until
1935, when it replaced an
earlier hostelry called the
Princess Helena. Legend
insists that the name
recalls a real donkey with
an exceptionally loud
bray, which lived in a
field opposite.

◄ **Holland-on-Sea**
The Cliffs c1955 H177013
Like Frinton, Holland has crumbling cliffs. Their debris becomes Gunfleet Sand, four miles out to sea. The historian Philip Morant said that Holland was "much exposed to the blasts from the sea". These days, the town is a centre for sailing, powerboat racing and windsurfing, and the nearby marshes teem with birdlife.

◄ **Holland-on-Sea
The Dining Room
Oakwood Hall c1955**

H177007
The tables are set,
awaiting the hungry
diners, and coconut
matting covers an
undulating floor. The
Black Forest cuckoo
clock and the oak
beams give this room a
distinctly 'quaint' air.
No doubt it would have
appealed to the waves of
American tourists who
were starting to discover
Britain at this time.

Holland-on-Sea
Oakwood Hall c1955
H177010
With the holiday trade underway, some of Holland's older buildings mutated into guesthouses. Oakwood Hall's uneven roofline gives away its age. Otherwise, the monkey puzzle trees and the touchingly rustic archway bring it into the golden era of the British seaside holiday.

Great Holland
Main Road c1955 G274010
Great Holland is midway between Clacton and Frinton. It is a quiet village, though it once had a dairy, a bakery, a hat shop, an antique shop, and a bicycle repair shop. The building facing us is the Lion's Den, formerly the Red Lion, its name punning on the fact that it was once a Daniell's pub.

Great Holland
The Ship Inn c1955 G274013
The Ship was once famous for its quoits lawn. It hosted the annual Peachey Quoits Cup competition; Mr Peachey was the owner of some nurseries in the village. One wonders if the quoits were made at the local foundry, Ratcliff's, whose usual output was shears and other agricultural implements.

▼ **Thorpe-le-Soken**
The Village c1955 T253012

The 'Soken' means that the village was under the jurisdiction (or 'soke') of St Paul's Cathedral. Pictured here is the Bell Hotel, with the overhanging gable that is so characteristic of the Tudor era. Opposite is Loblollies tearooms, Austin's wireless supplies, and the ubiquitous signs for Wall's ice cream and Hovis.

▼ **Thorpe-le-Soken**
The Village c1955 T253003

Thorpe is a thoroughfare village between Weeley and Frinton. The Cobbold's house in the middle distance is the Maid's Head, which was once known as the Maidenhead. Both it and the Bell were offering "seawater baths" in the 18th century, the Maidenhead's being "under the supervision of the doctors".

▲ **Frinton-on-Sea**
The Greensward 1921
70300

Frinton, as a resort, was less than forty years old when this picture was taken. In 1885 the Marine & General Company purchased land here, and began building 'Frinton Haven', with market, pier, tidal basin and pleasure gardens. Several of these ideas, such as the pier, were later abandoned.

**Frinton-on-Sea
Zigzag Path 1921** 70296
Frinton developed in a
quieter manner than Clacton
or Walton, and it has always
had a rather genteel air. It is
certainly not overrun with
holidaymakers in this view.
In the distance is Walton
Pier and, nearer
to us, some of the 32
breakwaters installed to
protect Frinton from the
worst ravages of the sea.

Frinton-on-Sea
Beach and Huts 1921 70305
A group of children pose around a rock pool, with varying degrees of
stiffness. The panama hats and high stockings are typical of the early
1920s. The building looming on the left is the Grand Hotel, which was
built in 1896, and extended forty years later. The cliff shelter with the
clock has been replaced by a more up-to-date version.

Frinton-on-Sea, The Cliffs 1921 70293
By the 1920s, beach huts had largely supplanted bathing machines, and there was often a 'no hut, no bathe'
regulation. The photo shows how the cliff had been scooped away by successive landslips. Coastal erosion has
always hampered Frinton: its original Hall was washed away in 1720, and the site is now half a mile out to sea.

Frinton-on-Sea, The Beach Approach c1955 F53005
Frinton's front has never been home to the gaudier aspects of seaside development. The town has been content with
such pleasures as the rock gardens, which are on the left, where the thatched hut is. Such quietude has led celebrities,
over the decades, to buy holiday homes here: Winston Churchill and Douglas Fairbanks Jr, to name but two.

◄ **Frinton-on-Sea
Connaught Avenue
c1955** F53023
This was a nameless,
muddy track before the
railway came to Frinton,
and it later became
Station Road. In 1904,
the Duke of Connaught
stayed at the Grand Hotel,
whilst umpiring army
manoeuvres in the area.
The road took his name.
The clock tower belongs
to the Free Church, a
1912 building that gained
this handsome addition
in 1935.

Frinton-on-Sea
The Greensward c1955

F53025

This photograph was clearly taken on a windy day - look at those trees. After the Frinton Sea Defence Act of 1901, the front was turfed and made into the Greensward. It had previously been a stretch of pastureland, which was used for grazing sheep and holding sports meetings. Frinton's footballers and cricketers subsequently found more permanent, if less dramatic, pitches.

Frinton-on-Sea
The Cliffs showing
Walton Pier c1955

F53029

This beach is a Mecca for fossil-hunters, as well as bathers. New finds are always being uncovered by erosion. Just north of here, a building called Burnt House Farm finally went over the cliff edge in 1899, even though, seventy years earlier, three fields had stood between it and the sea.

Frinton-on-Sea
The Cliffs from the
North c1955 F53028

This view is of an idyllic looking day, with sun on the water, and an uncrowded beach. The buildings on the cliff represent Frinton Park Estate. This scheme, devised in 1934, was set to incorporate houses, shops, churches and a hotel. Once the houses were built, there was little demand for them, and the project died a death.

◄ **Walton-on-the-Naze From the Pier 1894**

33972

In the 1820s, the Society of Friends at Colchester began to turn the farming village of Walton-le-Soken into the coastal resort of Walton-on-the-Naze. The row in the foreground, Marine Terrace, included a milliner's, a branch of the Essex & Suffolk Fire Office, and an outlet for groceries and 'fancy goods'. It is now Bruff Terrace.

◀ **Walton-on-the-Naze
The Pier 1891** 28237
Walton once had two
piers. The first, which
was built in 1830, was
washed away after fifty
years. This one, built
in 1870, was evidently
somewhat hardier, and it
appears to be well worth
the admission fee of 1d
a day. In the foreground,
we can just read that
one of the boats, the
'Mystery' of Walton, was
'licensed to carry 14'.

▼ **Walton-on-the-Naze
High Street and Church
1898** 41300
All Saints' church, seen
here, had replaced Walton's
medieval church, which
was consumed by the sea
in 1796. It had stood just
north of where the pier is.
The thatched building was
previously the Hoy, an
18th-century hostelry with
the obligatory smuggling
connections. Along the road
is the shop of H James,
confectioner and baker.

◀ **Walton-on-the-Naze
High Cliffe Mansion 1898**
41305
This house, originally known
as St Osyth's Home For Girls,
was built in the 1880s. It
later advertised itself as a
residential hotel with a large
garden and tennis courts. It
is now called Mabel Greville.
Knowing the instability of
Walton's cliffs, which is
fairly self-evident in this
photograph, one fears for the
future of this poor building.

◄ **Walton-on-the-Naze The Parade 1900** 45142
Initially, Walton's visitors were the 'better sort' of people. But, with the coming of the railway in 1867, the town was opened up to all. This picture includes hotels and 'dining & tea rooms' that catered for the influx. The rough area where the ladies are promenading is The Green: the closest Walton came to Frinton's Greensward.

◄ **Walton-on-the-Naze Shore Road 1900**

45141

The sea wall, only ten years old here, was never really high enough to contain the waves. This was particularly unfortunate for the Bath House Hotel (the first building along the road), which got a regular flushing-out from the sea. Charles Bates's bathing machines are in evidence here, although nobody is bathing.

▼ **Walton-on-the-Naze The Pier 1900** 45144

During the 1890s, the pier had had various structures added on. In the foreground, on the right, is the shooting saloon. Immediately beyond is the headquarters of Walton Swimming Club. Out on the pier-head, the Pavilion provided refreshments and daily entertainments, whilst the Belle Steamers arrived here once a day from London.

◄ **Walton-on-the-Naze From the Pier-Head 1900** 45143A

At 2,610 ft long, this was the second longest pier in England. A railway was installed on it in 1898 (note the carriages and bogie in the foreground) and kept going, with various revamps, until quite recently. Walton's seafront, seen here, has never quite lost its stately old-fashioned charm.

Walton-on-the-Naze From the Air 1954 AFA54834

◄ **Dovercourt**
Cliff Road 1894 33406
John Bagshaw, an East India merchant and, from 1847, MP for Harwich, saw the potential of Dovercourt as a resort. His plans initially centred on a spa-house, which opened in 1854 but did not last. Cliff Road dates from the following decade. It was a wide street, and consisted largely of lodging houses and homes for well-to-do professionals.

◀ Walton-on-the-Naze
The Beach c1955 W18018
Compare this with the shot of the beach in 1900. Here it is a forest of deckchairs, with cars parked bumper-to-bumper on the esplanade. Beachwear includes blazers for men, ribbons for small girls, and ruched bathing costumes. Beyond White Lodge lies the relative wilderness of the Naze itself - cliffs, marshes and quiet.

▼ Dovercourt
High Street c1950
D51005
There are least three signs for Hovis in this picture. Opposite the Co-op (which displays two of them) is George Smith's shop, 'growers of flowers and fruit'. Smith, a market gardener, had it purpose-built in 1898, to sell his produce. His nursery, he claimed, boasted 10,000 acres of glass.

◀ Dovercourt
High Street c1955
D51029
The property with the distinctive turret was built in 1902 by the Dovercourt & Harwich Co-operative Society. As well as their store, it also housed a billiards room, a reading room and a concert hall. At this time, the buildings on the right were still private residences. By 1905 they were converted into shops, including Went's shoes.

Dovercourt, The Promenade c1955 D51035
Notwithstanding its failure as a spa, Dovercourt did reasonably well as a modest seaside resort. Its attractions included a pair of 6-legged moveable lighthouses, one pictured here, and one a little further out to sea, which was linked to the first by a causeway. They were erected in 1863, and were in use until 1917.

Dovercourt, The Cliff Pavilion c1955 D51023
A bandstand was built here in 1902. Exposed to the elements, it was provided with a shelter, and evolved into the Cliff Pavilion. It had a large floor space, which was perfect for dances and concerts. The bulky shapes on the headland are part of Beacon Hill Battery, a derelict emplacement from the Second World War. Just inland is Queen Victoria's statue.

Dovercourt, High Street c1965 D51055
Fashions are changing, dress is becoming more casual, hair is longer, and the men in the foreground are evidence of this. The shop behind them, Coopers, had once been the premises of C E Bates, 'photographic artist and frame-maker'. The building with the pinnacles and strapwork parapets was the Capital & Counties Bank, dating from 1902. There is a proliferation of high-street names here.

Harwich, Corporation Pier c1955 H150022
Harwich is a well-kept secret. Ferry passengers only get to see Parkeston Quay, two miles away; they never see the town. Corporation Pier, seen here, is better known as the Ha'penny Pier, after its original toll charge. A small ferry goes from here to Felixstowe. The gazebo-type structure is the original ticket office, which was built in 1854.

Harwich, King's Quay Street c1950 H150001
The house with the advertisements for Craven 'A' and Player's was formerly the Ship Inn, which was built in the early 19th century on land adjacent to the old shipyard. The yard (behind the photographer) is now Navyard Wharf, from which Harwich's commercial traffic still departs. Further down the street, the Globe pre-dates the Ship by 300 years.

Harwich
The High Lighthouse c1955 H150018
A nine-sided tower of white brick, the High Lighthouse is Harwich's most striking feature. It was constructed in 1818 by civil engineer John Rennie Sr, although there had been a lighthouse on this spot since 1664. However, shifting sands meant the course of the channel changed, and the lighthouse was redundant by 1863.

Harwich, West Street c1950 H150007
Harwich is as 'olde worlde' as an Essex town gets. The streets retain a grid-like north-south pattern, with cross alleys staggered to break the strong easterly winds. West Street is largely Georgian. Halfway down, on the left, is the Elephant & Castle with its Dutch-style gable. Generations of Dutch immigrants had once disembarked at Harwich.

◄ **Mistley**
The Towers c1960
M131010
A new church was built at Mistley in 1735, after its medieval predecessor collapsed. Forty years later, the architect Robert Adam furnished it with twin towers as part of Richard Rigby's plans to upgrade the town. The towers were preserved as mausoleums when the body of the church was dismantled and sold for rubble in 1870.

◀ Harwich
West Street c1960
H150020
The man on the left is taking no chances, ladder wise. Nevertheless, the 1960s have arrived, and the shop on the right is now an agent for Vespa, prefiguring the surge of mods and rockers onto Essex's coastal scene. Harwich has the hallmarks of a once-prosperous town, and this it was, certainly up until the 18th century.

▼ Mistley
The Swan c1955 M131008
In the 18th century, two Richard Rigbys (father and son) began to develop Mistley as a model port. The younger was a notoriously extravagant Paymaster of the Forces under George III. He built new houses, granaries, warehouses and quays here. The centrepiece is this square with its porticoed malting office and water-gazing swan.

◀ Manningtree
River Stour c1955 M127019
The writer Reginald A Beckett visited this spot in 1901, and experienced only "the melancholy of treacherous green marsh and oozy mud". These days, it is really quite pleasant. Across the river in Brantham, Suffolk, is the 85-acre site of the British Xylonite Plastic Works, which has been established there since 1887.

115

Manningtree, Brook Street c1953 M127003
At 22 acres, Manningtree is the smallest parish in Essex, and also the smallest town in England. Small it may be, but it was famous for its good pasturage, which is why, we must assume, Shakespeare describes Falstaff as a "roasted Manningtree ox". The bunting in this picture suggests we are looking in on the town's Coronation festivities.

Manningtree, South Street c1955 M127021
Manningtree has a gradient that is rare in Essex towns. It also possesses a fine array of Georgian and Victorian frontages. Here we see, with the tobacco signs, Bertie Bullock's confectionery shop. A little further up is Calver & Arnold's clothiers and, displaying the banner for Murphy, Harwich Radio & Cycle Supplies.

Index

The Francis Frith Collection publishes over 100 new titles each year. A selection of those currently available is listed below. For latest catalogue please contact The Francis Frith Collection.
Town Books 96 pages, approximately 75 photos. **County and Themed Books** 128 pages, approximately 135 photos (unless specified). Pocket Albums are miniature editions of Frith local history books 128 pages, approximately 95 photos.

Accrington Old and New	Dorset Coast Pocket Album
Alderley Edge and Wilmslow	Dorset Living Memories
Amersham, Chesham and Rickmansworth	Dorset Villages
Andover	Down the Dart
Around Abergavenny	Down the Severn
Around Alton	Down the Thames
Aylesbury	Dunmow, Thaxted and Finchingfield
Barnstaple	Durham
Bedford	East Anglia Pocket Album
Bedfordshire	East Devon
Berkshire Living Memories	East Grinstead
Berkshire Pocket Album	Edinburgh
Blackpool Pocket Album	Ely and The Fens
Bognor Regis	Essex Pocket Album
Bournemouth	Essex Second Selection
Bradford	Essex: The London Boroughs
Bridgend	Exeter
Bridport	Exmoor
Brighton and Hove	Falmouth
Bristol	Farnborough, Fleet and Aldershot
Buckinghamshire	Folkestone
Calne Living Memories	Frome
Camberley Pocket Album	Furness and Cartmel Peninsulas
Canterbury Cathedral	Glamorgan
Cardiff Old and New	Glasgow
Chatham and the Medway Towns	Glastonbury
Chelmsford	Gloucester
Chepstow Then and Now	Gloucestershire
Cheshire	Greater Manchester
Cheshire Living Memories	Guildford
Chester	Hailsham
Chesterfield	Hampshire
Chigwell	Harrogate
Christchurch	Hastings and Bexhill
Churches of East Cornwall	Haywards Heath Living Memories
Clevedon	Heads of the Valleys
Clitheroe	Heart of Lancashire Pocket Album
Corby Living Memories	Helston
Cornish Coast	Herefordshire
Cornwall Living Memories	Horsham
Cotswold Living Memories	Humberside Pocket Album
Cotswold Pocket Album	Huntingdon, St Neots and St Ives
Coulsdon, Chipstead and Woodmanstern	Hythe, Romney Marsh and Ashford
County Durham	Ilfracombe
Cromer, Sheringham and Holt	Ipswich Pocket Album
Dartmoor Pocket Album	Isle of Wight
Derby	Isle of Wight Living Memories
Derbyshire	King's Lynn
Derbyshire Living Memories	Kingston upon Thames
Devon	Lake District Pocket Album
Devon Churches	Lancashire Living Memories
Dorchester	Lancashire Villages

Available from your local bookshop or from the publisher

The Francis Frith Collection Titles (continued)

Lancaster, Morecambe and Heysham Pocket Album
Leeds Pocket Album
Leicester
Leicestershire
Lincolnshire Living Memoires
Lincolnshire Pocket Album
Liverpool and Merseyside
London Pocket Album
Ludlow
Maidenhead
Maidstone
Malmesbury
Manchester Pocket Album
Marlborough
Matlock
Merseyside Living Memories
Nantwich and Crewe
New Forest
Newbury Living Memories
Newquay to St Ives
North Devon Living Memories
North London
North Wales
North Yorkshire
Northamptonshire
Northumberland
Northwich
Nottingham
Nottinghamshire Pocket Album
Oakham
Odiham Then and Now
Oxford Pocket Album
Oxfordshire
Padstow
Pembrokeshire
Penzance
Petersfield Then and Now
Plymouth
Poole and Sandbanks
Preston Pocket Album
Ramsgate Old and New
Reading Pocket Album
Redditch Living Memories
Redhill to Reigate
Richmond
Ringwood
Rochdale
Romford Pocket Album
Salisbury Pocket Album
Scotland
Scottish Castles
Sevenoaks and Tonbridge
Sheffield and South Yorkshire Pocket Album
Shropshire
Somerset
South Devon Coast
South Devon Living Memories
South East London

Southampton Pocket Album
Southend Pocket Album
Southport
Southwold to Aldeburgh
Stourbridge Living Memories
Stratford upon Avon
Stroud
Suffolk
Suffolk Pocket Album
Surrey Living Memories
Sussex
Sutton
Swanage and Purbeck
Swansea Pocket Album
Swindon Living Memories
Taunton
Teignmouth
Tenby and Saundersfoot
Tiverton
Torbay
Truro
Uppingham
Villages of Kent
Villages of Surrey
Villages of Sussex Pocket Album
Wakefield and the Five Towns Living Memories
Warrington
Warwick
Warwickshire Pocket Album
Wellingborough Living Memories
Wells
Welsh Castles
West Midlands Pocket Album
West Wiltshire Towns
West Yorkshire
Weston-super-Mare
Weymouth
Widnes and Runcorn
Wiltshire Churches
Wiltshire Living Memories
Wiltshire Pocket Album
Wimborne
Winchester Pocket Album
Windermere
Windsor
Wirral
Wokingham and Bracknell
Woodbridge
Worcester
Worcestershire
Worcestershire Living Memories
Wyre Forest
York Pocket Album
Yorkshire
Yorkshire Coastal Memories
Yorkshire Dales
Yorkshire Revisited

See Frith books on the internet at www.francisfrith.com

FRITH PRODUCTS & SERVICES

Francis Frith would doubtless be pleased to know that the pioneering publishing venture he started in 1860 still continues today. Over a hundred and forty years later, The Francis Frith Collection continues in the same innovative tradition and is now one of the foremost publishers of vintage photographs in the world. Some of the current activities include:

INTERIOR DECORATION

Today Frith's photographs can be seen framed and as giant wall murals in thousands of pubs, restaurants, hotels, banks, retail stores and other public buildings throughout the country. In every case they enhance the unique local atmosphere of the places they depict and provide reminders of gentler days in an increasingly busy and frenetic world.

PRODUCT PROMOTIONS

Frith products are used by many major companies to promote the sales of their own products or to reinforce their own history and heritage. Frith promotions have been used by Hovis bread, Courage beers, Scots Porage Oats, Colman's mustard, Cadbury's foods, Mellow Birds coffee, Dunhill pipe tobacco, Guinness, and Bulmer's Cider.

GENEALOGY AND FAMILY HISTORY

As the interest in family history and roots grows world-wide, more and more people are turning to Frith's photographs of Great Britain for images of the towns, villages and streets where their ancestors lived; and, of course, photographs of the churches and chapels where their ancestors were christened, married and buried are an essential part of every genealogy tree and family album.

FRITH PRODUCTS

All Frith photographs are available Framed or just as Mounted Prints and Posters (size 23 x 16 inches). These may be ordered from the address below. Other products available are- Address Books, Calendars, Jigsaws, Canvas Prints, Coasters, Notelets and local and prestige books.

THE INTERNET

Already ninety thousand Frith photographs can be viewed and purchased on the internet through the Frith websites and a myriad of partner sites.

For more detailed information on Frith companies and products, look at this site:
www.francisfrith.com

See the complete list of Frith Books at: www.francisfrith.com
This web site is regularly updated with the latest list of publications from The Francis Frith Collection. If you wish to buy books relating to another part of the country that your local bookshop does not stock, you may purchase on-line.

For further information, trade, or author enquiries please contact us at the address below:
The Francis Frith Collection, Frith's Barn, Teffont, Salisbury, Wiltshire, England SP3 5QP.
Tel: +44 (0)1722 716 376 Fax: +44 (0)1722 716 881 Email: sales@francisfrith.co.uk

See Frith products on the internet at www.francisfrith.com

FREE PRINT OF YOUR CHOICE

Mounted Print
Overall size 14 x 11 inches (355 x 280mm)

Choose any Frith photograph in this book.
Simply complete the Voucher opposite and return it with your remittance for £3.50 (to cover postage and handling) and we will print the photograph of your choice in SEPIA (size 11 x 8 inches) and supply it in a cream mount with a burgundy rule line (overall size 14 x 11 inches).
Please note: aerial photographs and photographs with a reference number starting with a "Z" are not Frith photographs and cannot be supplied under this offer. Offer valid for delivery to one UK address only.

PLUS: Order additional Mounted Prints at HALF PRICE - £9.50 each (normally £19.00)
If you would like to order more Frith prints from this book, possibly as gifts for friends and family, you can buy them at half price (with no additional postage and handling costs).

PLUS: Have your Mounted Prints framed
For an extra £18.00 per print you can have your mounted print(s) framed in an elegant polished wood and gilt moulding, overall size 16 x 13 inches (no additional postage and handling required).

IMPORTANT!

These special prices are only available if you use this form to order. You must use the ORIGINAL VOUCHER on this page (no copies permitted). We can only despatch to one UK address. This offer cannot be combined with any other offer.

Send completed Voucher form to:
The Francis Frith Collection, Frith's Barn, Teffont, Salisbury, Wiltshire SP3 5QP

CHOOSE A PHOTOGRAPH FROM THIS BOOK

Voucher for **FREE** *and Reduced Price Frith Prints*

Please do not photocopy this voucher. Only the original is valid, so please fill it in, cut it out and return it to us with your order.

Picture ref no	Page no	Qty	Mounted @ £9.50	Framed + £18.00	Total Cost £
		1	Free of charge*	£	£
			£9.50	£	£
			£9.50	£	£
			£9.50	£	£
			£9.50	£	£
			£9.50	£	£
Please allow 28 days for delivery. Offer available to one UK address only			* Post & handling		£3.50
			Total Order Cost		£

Title of this book . . . .

I enclose a cheque/postal order for £ . . . . made payable to 'The Francis Frith Collection'

OR please debit my Mastercard / Visa / Maestro card, details below

Card Number

Issue No (Maestro only)   Valid from (Maestro)

Expires   Signature

Name Mr/Mrs/Ms . . . .
Address . . . .
. . . .
. . . .
. . . . Postcode . . . .
Daytime Tel No . . . .
Email . . . .

978-1-84589-448-1   Valid to 31/12/11

Can you help us with information about any of the Frith photographs in this book?

We are gradually compiling an historical record for each of the photographs in the Frith archive. It is always fascinating to find out the names of the people shown in the pictures, as well as insights into the shops, buildings and other features depicted.

If you recognize anyone in the photographs in this book, or if you have information not already included in the author's caption, do let us know. We would love to hear from you, and will try to publish it in future books or articles.

An Invitation from The Francis Frith Collection to Share Your Memories

The 'Share Your Memories' feature of our website allows members of the public to add personal memories relating to the places featured in our photographs, or comment on others already added. Seeing a place from your past can rekindle forgotten or long held memories. Why not visit the website, find photographs of places you know well and add YOUR story for others to read and enjoy? We would love to hear from you!

www.francisfrith.com/memories

Our production team

Frith books are produced by a small dedicated team at offices in the converted Grade II listed 18th-century barn at Teffont near Salisbury, illustrated above. Most have worked with the Frith Collection for many years. All have in common one quality: they have a passion for the Frith Collection.

Frith Books and Gifts

We have a wide range of books and gifts available on our website utilising our photographic archive, many of which can be individually personalised.

www.francisfrith.com